Fresh Creations presents...

Food for Your Thoughts...

It all started with the basic food groups...

"Food 101-*Always Eat Fresh! To be a chef you must believe you are a new culinary master who is not afraid to use new and intriguing ingredients. Don't fear new recipes, it is always good to spice up life with some flair and a little attitude. So grab an apron, a knife and your thinking cap...it is time to have* **Food for Your Thoughts" –LG.**

So let's talk about food, do you fear your kitchen or do you find yourself utilizing the same ingredients *night after night*? It's time to think on your feet, use ingredients you enjoy and combine them with something new!

Hmm...it's easy to think on your feet but what happens when you *can't balance?*

Some of us love food but struggle with the preparation and flavors of our masterpieces. **It is simple, keep practicing...**

Try a *simple* recipe:

Fantastic French Toast (serves 2 to 3)
2 eggs
8 slices of bread (white or wheat)
½ c. Milk
2 T. Orange Liqueur
Mix **eggs, milk and orange liqueur**, dip bread in batter. Heat frying pan to medium heat, drop battered bread onto pan. Flip generously for even cooking and a delicious breakfast. Place on plate, add butter and sprinkle confectioners' sugar. Top with Syrup to taste.

Voile! Your first culinary masterpiece, **if you burnt the first batch don't feel disappointed,** each stove will be different for temperatures. *Try lowering the heat next time*!

Food is a funny thing, we all need it to survive but only some of us are lucky enough to be culinary masters. In this cookbook you will learn to find your own specialty in the kitchen.
Through the years, food has had many *looks*, **styles** and <u>variations</u> but it has always brought family and friends together to share in **delicious food and great memories.**

Some smells connect a place and time for many of us, like Mom's kitchen or the local deli around the corner. We all have a soft spot for favorites, giving us the warm feeling of comfort.

Feeling home sick? Easy recipes are rewarding and delicious!

Bring some goodness to lunch time or when you are on the run!

Grand Grilled Cheese

Cheddar cheese, sliced
Mozzarella cheese, sliced
2 T. butter
2 slices of bacon
2 slices of tomato
Wheat, white, or rye bread, 2 slices

Frying pan=Medium heat. Butter one side of each slice of bread. Add cheese, bacon and tomato. Flip generously. **Watch the temperature, butter burns fast!**

Don't forget you can use American cheese too!

Garlic Toast

Italian bread loaf
2 garlic clove, minced
Salt/Pepper
2 T. olive oil
4 T. pecorino romano cheese
1 c. grated mozzarella

Oven=350 degrees. Place bread on foil; add olive oil, salt, pepper, garlic, and cheeses. Cook for 10-15 minutes. Cut into slices and serve.

Get sassy! *Use garlic toast for the ultimate grilled cheese and enjoy a scrumptious delight!*

Food for the Road...

Tempting Tuna (serves 2 to 3)
1 7oz. can Tuna (solid white albacore in water)
2 T. mayo
2 tsp. spicy or yellow mustard
Salt/Pepper/Garlic Powder
1 T. sweet relish
Wheat or white bread
Romaine lettuce leaves
1 Apple-cut into 12 to15 pieces

Drain tuna. Add mayo, mustard, salt, pepper, garlic powder, & sweet relish. Mix and scoop onto bread.

Apple on the side to balance the sweet and salty lunch craving!

Lunch and Munch

<u>CooCoo Chickadee Salad(serves 2 to 3)</u>
1 c. boneless chicken breast, chopped
2 T. mayo
1 tsp. mustard
¼ c. celery, diced
½ c. green or red grapes, sliced in half
Salt/pepper/garlic and onion powder
Combine chopped chicken with mayo, mustard, salt, pepper, garlic and onion powder, celery and grapes. Mix and Stuff it in pita!

Sweet & Simple:

<u>Mid-Day Snack</u>
Rice cakes, 2
2 T. Nutella spread
1 Banana
Smother rice cake with Nutella spread, slice banana on top. Mmm!

Feel yourself zoning out? Try a Green apple for a Zing!

Spice up your life! Social gatherings always need a great start to kick off the evening.

Events can pop up last minute so make something that will be a hit without all the extra preparation and time!

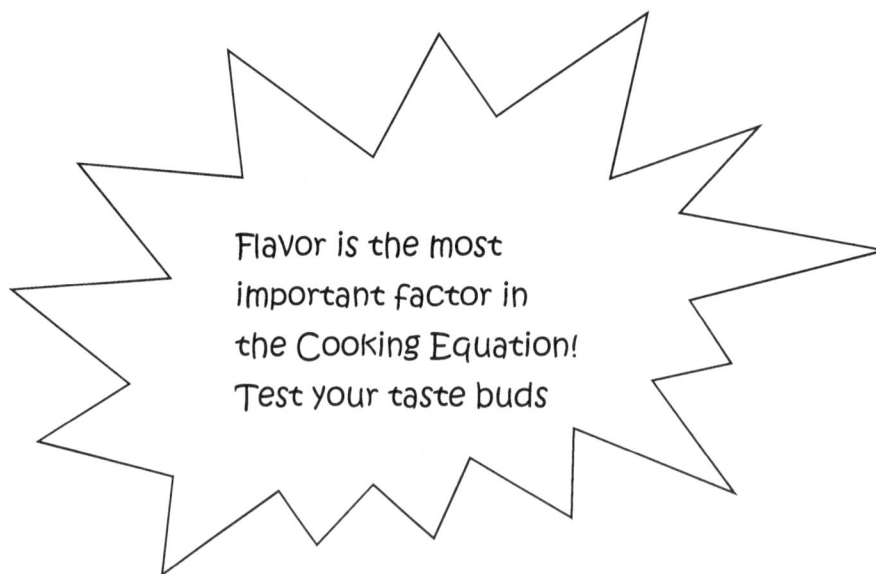

Flavor is the most important factor in the Cooking Equation! Test your taste buds

Forgot about the last minute **Friday Night Party**?

Sassy Sangria

1 jug of red wine
½ c. sugar
4 c. orange juice
2 c. pineapple juice or apple juice
2 c. tequila
½ liter of ginger ale
2 navel oranges
2 apples, of choice
Dice oranges and apples, place in a bowl and add ingredients!
Add ice and serve!

Caution!
Very Strong!
Drink with Friends

Corny Guacamole

1 can of golden corn, drained
Cilantro, finely chopped
Salt/ pepper
¼ c. lime juice
3 avocados, diced
1 small red onion, diced
Combine avocado with lime juice, corn, onion and seasonings.

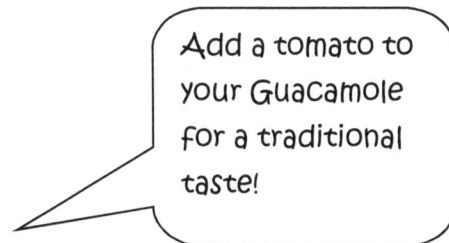

Add a tomato to your Guacamole for a traditional taste!

Fun and Festive

Fiesta Dip
1 can of black beans, drained
1 can of garbanzo beans, drained
1 green pepper, chopped
2 tomatoes, chopped
1 can of golden corn, drained
1 small onion, chopped
½ c. red wine vinegar
¼ c. oil
1 garlic clove, minced
Cilantro, minced
1 tsp. red pepper flakes
1 T. Adobo seasoning
1 or 2 limes, squeezed
Combine all ingredients into a bowl. Chill and serve with chips!

Don't forget, all spices are to your own taste. *Feel free to add more spice to your dishes!*

Salsa Fresca

3 tomatoes, chopped
Cilantro, finely chopped
Salt/pepper
1 tsp. red pepper flakes
1 clove garlic, minced
½ c. white vinegar
¼ c. olive oil
1 green pepper, diced
1 yellow onion, chopped
Combine all ingredients in a small bowl.

Make your own Tortilla Chips:
3 white flour tortillas
Add olive oil and salt
Slice like pizza &
 Bake at 350 degrees for
5 minutes.

Fabulously Fruity

1 can black beans, drained
2 mango, chopped
1 can crushed pineapple, drained
Cilantro, minced
Salt/pepper
2 T. vegetable oil
¼ c. red wine vinegar
1 lime, squeezed
Combine mango, beans, pineapple then add vinegar, lime, oil and cilantro. Add in seasonings and mix well.
Serve with yellow corn chips for zest.

For an extra kick, add Hot Peppers!

Remember when you would sit in your Grandmother's kitchen just waiting for that delicious smell lingering to enter your belly? **Well now you can get that home cooking you have been drooling over**...

Test your skills, you can do this!

Take it to the next level, Breathe and let's try something new!

Your greatest hit...

<u>Sweet and Simple Tea</u>
¼ c. mint leaves, crushed
4 c. boiling water
5 tea bags (black tea)
½ c. natural sugar
Boil water, add tea bags and mint leaves.
Add ice for a refreshing and tasty treat!

Brew tea for 3-7 minutes...some like teas strong!

<u>Simple syrup</u>
1 c. organic or natural sugar
1 c. water
Boil and stir until *dissolved.*

Now that you are refreshed...
Roll up your sleeves and **get down to food...**

For starters:

Mama's Mashed Potatoes
10-15 red potatoes
2 T. salt
½ stick of Butter
½ c. milk
Garlic powder
Pepper
Boil water with potatoes, add salt twice.
Strain potatoes, mash then add butter, milk, garlic powder, pepper and more salt if needed.

Mashed potatoes can never be over mashed, get that frustration out!

Time to Impress the Family...

London broil Bridges

3 lbs. London broil
½ c red wine vinegar
4 T. ketchup
2 cloves fresh garlic, minced
Salt/pepper/onion powder
2 T. soy sauce
1 tsp. Adobo seasoning (tenderizer)
1 T. oil
Italian seasonings
Medium heat=stove top
Combine all ingredients and marinate in refrigerator for 1 hour.
Braise on stove top! Cook time based on temperature selection.

15 minutes for Medium rare- 30 minutes for Medium well

Baked Veggie Blast

1 zucchini, sliced
2 carrots, peeled and cut into strips
1 squash, sliced
2 T. olive oil
Salt/pepper/garlic powder
¼ c. breadcrumbs, Italian seasoned
Pecorino Romano cheese
Oven=350 degrees. Place veggies on a pan, drizzle with oil, cheese and seasonings. Bake for 15-20 minutes and serve!

Turn up the Flavor!

<u>Garlic Mayo</u>
Parsley flakes
1 T. olive oil
½ c. mayo
1 clove garlic, minced
Blend in food processor, chill and serve!

Try Garlic Mayo on the London broil

Food for your Thought:
"Things are only as impossible as you make them."

Sassin' up the Sauces...

Sunday's Secret Sauce

2 large cans, crushed tomatoes
1 large can, chunky crushed tomatoes
2 cloves of garlic, pressed
3 or 4 basil leaves, chopped
Salt/pepper/garlic and onion powder
Italian seasonings, dried
2 T. olive oil
½ c. red wine

Stove=Low Heat

Heat pot with olive oil and pressed garlic. Add cans of tomatoes then all spices and herbs, add wine. **Cook for at least 1 hour**, stir frequently. *Watch the bottom does not stick!*

Fabulous Flavors

Serve with Penne, Rigatoni, or Angel hair...*Don't forget the grated cheese!*

"The best way to succeed is to take action."

Sweet and Spicy Sauce
2 T. oil
Salt/pepper
½ tsp. red pepper flakes
1 clove garlic, pressed
¼ c. sugar
1 T. grape jelly
1 T. red wine vinegar
Simmer on low heat, stir until smooth.

Great for marinades, try it on grilled shrimp skewers!

Ridiculous Relish
1 red pepper, diced
1 cucumber, minced
½ c. red wine vinegar
Salt
¼ c. sugar
Blend in processor and chill

Fair Food for You...
Great on the classic hotdog!

Dinner bell is ringing...
Even your boss would be impressed

Award winning Ribs
1 package baby back pork ribs
1 T. mustard
3 T. ketchup
1 c. barbeque sauce
½ c. hot sauce
Salt/pepper/garlic powder
Parsley flakes
¼ c. red wine vinegar
¼ c. oil
2 T. honey
Smother ribs with ingredients, let marinate for 30-45 minutes in refrigerator.
Grill on medium heat for 20-25 minutes, or Bake on 400 for 20 minutes. *These tend to dry out, so watch the temperature.*

Extra napkins will be necessary!

Time for Dinner, you forgot to pull something out of the freezer to defrost. Now you only have an hour and little patience to create a culinary masterpiece!

Some of the best dinners you can make are in this cookbook, and within your financial budget!

Take a chance and mix up some ingredients. Once you are comfortable with cooking, flavors and ingredients become natural!

Quick and Easy

Tasty Turkey Tacos

2 lbs. ground turkey meat, lean
½ packet of taco seasoning
½ c. ketchup
¼ c. oil
1 T. hot sauce
½ c. water, as needed
Garlic and onion powder

Bake turkey meat in a pan, 350 degrees for 10 minutes. *In a sauce pan add water, oil, ketchup, taco seasoning and hot sauce to turkey meat on medium heat.* **Cook for 15 minutes**. Stir frequently.

...with Fixin's on the side

1 8 oz. cheddar cheese, grated
¼ head of Iceberg lettuce, shredded
Fresh (pg. 6) salsa or store bought salsa
Taco sauce
Hard shells/Soft wraps

Family Favorites...

Chunky and Funky Chili

2 green peppers, diced
1 medium can, diced tomatoes
1 large can, crushed tomatoes
1 small can, tomato paste
1 large can, kidney beans
2 lbs. ground beef 80/20 lean
2 T. Adobo seasoning
1 onion, chopped
Salt/pepper
1 T. Red pepper flakes
1 clove of garlic, pressed
2 T. vegetable oil

Bake ground beef on 350 for 15 minutes.
Add oil and garlic to large pot on medium heat, and then add peppers, onions and beef. Combine both cans of tomatoes, paste, kidney beans and all seasonings. Cook on medium heat for at least 2 hours. *Hot sauce may be added to kick up the heat!*

Mmm, *no chili is complete without some chips and sour cream!*

Staying Fresh...

The best part of about cooking is the fresh ingredients we use to create culinary masterpieces. It is important to be selective of quality versus price of items. *Just because one brand is more expensive, does not mean it will taste any better!*

Add Zest to your life!

Stay fresh and enjoy your masterpieces!

Heating up!

<u>Savory Swordfish</u>
Swordfish steaks
Salt/pepper/parsley flakes
½ c. lemon juice, per taste
2 T. olive oil
Grill on medium setting for about 10-12 minutes, flip generously.
Or Broil in the oven for 5-7 minutes on each side!

<u>Classy Chicken Skewers</u>
3 lbs. boneless chicken breasts, strips
½ c. lime juice
2 large yellow onion, cut into slices
Salt/pepper
2 T. olive oil
2 green/red peppers, sliced
¼ c. Tequila
Grill=Medium heat
Toss chicken strips and vegetables ALL seasoning.
Cook until juices run clear!
Feel free to be Fresh...

Lime Dipping Sauce:
2 limes, squeezed
Cilantro, finely chopped
Salt/pepper/garlic powder
1 cucumber, diced
1 c. plain yogurt
Blend all ingredients in

Cool and Fresh...

<u>Fresh Salad</u>
3 c. watermelon
2 tomatoes, sliced thin
½ c. feta cheese
1 yellow tomato (in season)
2 c. arugula
2 T. olive oil
Salt/Pepper
Combine arugula, watermelon, tomato and feta on a plate.
Drizzle oil, salt and pepper across the plate for taste.

Great for spring or summer dinner!

<u>Ritzy Rice Salad</u>
1 can corn, roasted
Salt/pepper
1 pkg. cherry tomatoes, sliced in half
1 cucumber, diced
2 c. rice, cooked
2 T. olive oil
¼ c. lemon juice
2 tsp. Dijon mustard
Combine all ingredients in a bowl and serve!

Sweet & Simple...

Fresh Cream
1 c. heavy cream
1 T. butter
1 tsp. vanilla flavor
Beat and set in refrigerator.

Keep it simple, less is more when it comes to food!

Crazy for Coconut
1 c. shredded coconut
1 T. honey
2 tsp. cinnamon
½ c. almond slices
Toss coconut, almonds, honey and cinnamon. Toast in oven on 250 degrees for 5-7 minutes. **Watch these will burn quickly!**

Wow your Guests,
serve something
sensational to satisfy
that sweet tooth!

If your diet is specific...
Try these desserts with Frozen Yogurt
or Sugar-free sauces!

Tantalizing Treats...

Graciously Great Granola

¼ c. sugar
1 T. honey
1 T. cinnamon
½ c. oats, uncooked
¼ c. almond slices
¼ c. raisins
¼ c. craisins
5-7 graham crackers, crushed
Toss all ingredients together, **toast for 5 minutes!**

Perfect for in between snacks! Travels well, too!

Just Peachy

4 peaches, cut into halves
½ c. brown sugar or natural sugar
1 tsp. cinnamon
Lightly sprinkle sugar and cinnamon onto peach halves. Grill on low heat for about 5-7 minutes.
Do not remove skins, this will help while grilling.
Serve with vanilla ice cream.

Caramel sauce drizzled onto ice cream for a zing!

Tasty Tricks...

<u>Late Night Breakfast</u>
2 c. biscuit mix
1 egg
½ c. vegetable oil
1 1/3 c. club soda
In a bowl combine all ingredients, turn waffle maker on. *Pour batter into waffle maker and flip.*
Top waffles with 1 scoop of vanilla and 1 scoop of chocolate ice cream. Drizzle with chocolate syrup or strawberry sauce.

Didn't use all the waffle batter? *Save it in the freezer for up to 1 week.*

Use it at Breakfast for a head start!

Time to Cleanse your Palette...

Lemon Sorbet
½ C. lemon juice
2 C. water
¼ C. sugar
Lemon rinds
Combine ingredients.
Set in bowl and freeze.

Try this Recipe with Lime or any other type of Citrus fruit for an extra Zing!

Feels like Fall...

Fall Fiesta Queso

1 zucchini or squash, cooked
1 can corn, drained
Cilantro, finely chopped
½ c. jalapeno, chopped
1 c. jack cheese, grated
Sautee zucchini first then combine all other ingredients into a sauce pan. **Simmer on medium heat until smooth.**

Apple Crumble

6-8 gala apples, slices
1 c. sugar
1 T. cinnamon
¼ c. lemon juice
½ c. sliced almonds
2 tsp. vanilla or rum extract
1 tsp. salt
1 T. honey
Premade crust

Don't forget the best part, *make it a la mode*...with vanilla ice cream!

Toss apples with all ingredients. Place into premade crust.
In a separate bowl, add *1 stick of butter, ½ c. flour, ¼ c. brown sugar, 1 tsp. cinnamon. Use a fork to push all ingredients into small piles. Crumble this on top of apples.*
Oven=350 for about 35-40 minutes.

Now that you have finished all your tests, how do you feel? *You are now a culinary master of your own kitchen.*

Are you surprised at how well you've done? *Don't be!* You deserve a break now that you have impressed yourself.

Keep life simple. Enjoy the little things...
Sit down with a *hot Green Tea*, **add some of your simple syrup and relax.**

And remember to
"Always Eat Fresh"

www.ingramcontent.com/pod-product-compliance
Lightning Source LLC
Chambersburg PA
CBHW061354090426
42739CB00002B/30